I0762653

Little Mitchie
IT TASTES
SAVORY
LET'S LEARN ABOUT
FLAVORS
Kim Thompson

CREATING YOUNG NONFICTION READERS

Little Mitchie books spark curiosity and support early nonfiction reading for students in Grades 2-3. Designed to build vocabulary, support second language learners, and prepare readers for middle-grade content, each book includes helpful tips for parents and educators to build confidence and deepen understanding of the world.

TIPS FOR READING NONFICTION WITH BEGINNING READERS

Talk about Nonfiction

Begin by explaining that nonfiction books give us information that is true. The book will be organized around a specific topic or idea, and we may learn new facts through reading.

Look at the Parts

Most nonfiction books have helpful features. Our *Little Mitchie* titles include color photographs and graphic aids, a table of contents, a glossary, and an index. Share the purpose of these features with your reader.

Color Photos and Graphic Aids

A lot of information can be found by "reading" photos, charts, maps, and other graphic aids found within nonfiction texts. Help your reader learn more about the different ways information can be displayed.

Table of Contents

Located at the front of the book, this list shows the big ideas within the text and the page numbers where they can be found.

Glossary

Located at the back of the book, the glossary defines key words and phrases that are related to the topic. These words and phrases can be found in the text in colored type.

Index

Located at the back of the book, an index is an alphabetical list of topics and the page numbers where they can be found.

With a little help and guidance about reading nonfiction, you can feel good about introducing a young reader to the world of *Little Mitchie* nonfiction books.

Little Mitchie is an imprint of:

Mitchell Lane
PUBLISHERS

2001 SW 31st Avenue
Hallandale, FL 33009
mitchelllanepub.com

First Edition, 2027.

Author: Kim Thompson
Designer: Bobbie Houser

Library of Congress Cataloging-in-Publication Data
Title: It Tastes Savory / by Kim Thompson

Description: Hallandale, FL :
Mitchell Lane Publishers, [2027]

Identifiers:
ISBN 979-8-89260-856-5 (library bound)
ISBN 979-8-89260-953-1 (eBook)

Library of Congress Control Number: 2026935891

PHOTO CREDITS
Dreamstime: Juliarstudio, cover, 1, 3, 4, 10, 18; Shutterstock: Vladislav Chusov, 5; SabbirDigitalll, 7; siamionau pavel, 8; Alex_Karlssonn, 9; suriya yapin, 11; New Africa, 13; polinaloves, 15; AYO Production, 16; Chubykin Arkady, 19; DEB SUMON, 20; SV_Digital_Press, 22.

TABLE OF CONTENTS

Chapter One

A SAVORY TASTE

Imagine a meal of noodles, meat, mushrooms, beans, and garlic. Before digging in, you add a splash of soy sauce.

The foods in the bowl have different shapes, colors, and textures. They have one flavor in common, though. They are all savory!

Savory foods are all around us. Some can be harvested from the garden. Corn, tomatoes, and potatoes are savory. So are spinach, carrots, and nuts.

Some savory foods come from stoves, ovens, and woks. Cooking releases savoriness. It **enhances** the flavor.

Think of lasagna, **miso soup**, or stew. These dishes contain savory foods like beef, fish, seaweed, and cheese. Cooked with other ingredients, they are extra delicious.

Chapter Two

THE SCIENCE OF SAVORINESS

Savory tastes are deep and complex. They are meaty and **luscious**. They come from foods rich in **amino acids** such as glutamate. Savory foods also contain nucleotides, which are found in **DNA**.

TASTY TIDBIT
Japanese scientist Kikunae Ikeda discovered glutamate. He invented the artificial form shown here. It is called MSG. It is used to enhance the flavor of foods.

Bumps called **papillae** cover your tongue. Don't mistake these for taste buds. Taste buds are tiny structures inside papillae.

Taste buds are shaped like pockets. Tiny hairs called microvilli stick out. Microvilli sense amino acids. They sense nucleotides. They send **signals** to the brain. That's how you can tell you are tasting something savory.

TASTY TIDBIT

Savory foods really are mouthwatering. Tasting them makes people produce more saliva.

TASTY TIDBIT

People used to think that different areas of your tongue tasted different flavors. That's not true. All five flavors can be sensed all over your tongue.

Five flavors can be sensed by your taste buds. Savory is one. The others are sweet, salty, sour, and bitter.

Younger people have more taste buds than older people. That's why flavors often taste stronger to kids than they do to adults.

TASTY TIDBIT
When you have a cold, your nose is less sensitive to smells. It is more difficult to taste your food.

There is another body part that can taste. It's your nose! When you chew, food smells travel up your nose. Sense **receptors** are activated. They send messages to your brain about flavor.

Chapter Three

EATING SAVORY FOODS

Our bodies need **protein**. It is found in meat and other savory foods. That could be why humans are able to taste savory flavors. It helps us detect protein sources that we need to live.

Savory foods are yummy. They are also good for you. Go ahead and enjoy your favorite cheesy, nutty, and meaty meals. They make you happy and healthy.

UMAMI PIZZA

Ingredients:

One store-bought pizza crust

One jar pizza sauce

Two cups shredded mozzarella or other cheese

Your choice of savory toppings, such as pepperoni or other meats, parmesan cheese, mushrooms, chopped tomatoes, garlic, dried seaweed, almonds, sun-dried tomatoes, spinach, or anchovies

Directions:

1. Ask an adult to help you preheat the oven according to the directions on the crust package.
2. Spread sauce on the crust. Sprinkle on cheese. Then, add as many of the toppings as you like.
3. Bake the pizza according to the directions on the crust package. Allow to cool slightly before slicing.
4. Eat and enjoy! Talk about which savory toppings you like best.

GLOSSARY

amino acids (uh-MEE-noh AS-ids) chemicals that make up proteins

DNA (DEE-en-ay) groups of chemicals that are found inside the cells of living things and that carry genetic information; deoxyribonucleic acid

enhances (en-HAN-sis) makes something bigger or better

luscious (LUH-shuhs) having a delicious taste or smell

miso soup (MEE-soh soop) a traditional Japanese soup made from fish, seaweed, tofu, green onions, and other ingredients

papillae (puh-PILL-ee) small bumps on the tongue that contain taste buds

protein (PROH-teen) a chemical compound found in living things and in foods such as meat, cheese, fish, eggs, and beans

receptors (ri-SEP-turz) nerve endings that are sensitive to stimuli in the environment such as smells

saliva (suh-LYE-vuh) the watery fluid that keeps your mouth moist and that helps you soften and digest food

signals (SIG-nuhlz) chemical and electrical messages that get sent to the brain through the body's nervous system

FURTHER READING

Grant, Jacob. *Umami.* Viking Books for Young Readers, 2024.

Highlights. *The Ultimate Science Cookbook for Kids: A Cookbook for Young Scientists That Transforms the Kitchen into a Food Lab for Learning.* Highlights Press, 2025.

ON THE INTERNET

PBS: Serving Up Science: Umami: The Fifth Taste
pbs.org/video/when-did-umami-join-sweet-sour-bitter-and-salty-ef3ytw
Learn the history and science behind savory tastes.

SciShow Kids: Your Tongue: The Taste-Maker!
youtube.com/watch?v=C4rdqXXzPGU
Learn how your tongue, nose, and brain work together to help you taste.

INDEX